ONCE A UPON A MIDNIGHT CLEAR.........

GOD's Love For US. . . .

(JEREMIAH 29:11)
" FOR I KNOW THE PLANS I HAVE FOR YOU,"

**DECLARES THE "LORD,"
"PLANS TO PROSPER YOU AND NOT HARM YOU,
"PLANS TO GIVE YOU HOPE AND A FUTURE!"**

Prayer & Meditation Plan of Restoration

" I must live with a repentant heart, my mind is renewed! I want my thoughts to be truthful , I want my ways to be true and loving in all my ways…Please forgive me of anger, forgive me of all that I have done wrong against heaven. Please forgive them who harbor unforgiving hearts against heaven. I release anger, frustration and confusion. I replace it with the compassion of love, which flows from my heart and I will continue to have love for others Because I know that forgiveness, relieves pain. confess this to be the true in the name of fellowship for humanity from this day forward I, let it go now and forever! Other people's actions, words and deeds no longer matter, I give it all to the heavens' I pray that fear will no long hold me hostage" FEAR is: False Evidence Appearing Real

WORDS OF WISDOM

"There comes a time in your life when you finally get it... When in the midst of all your fears and insanity you stop dead in your tracks and somewhere the voice inside your head cries out ENOUGH!

Enough fighting and crying or struggling to hold on

And, like a child quieting down after a blind tantrum, your sobs begin to subside, you shudder once or twice, you blink back your tears and through a mantle of wet lashes you begin to look at the world from a new perspective.

This is your awakening. . . . .
You realize that it is time to stop hoping and waiting for something or someone to change, or for happiness safety and security to come galloping over the next horizon.
You come to terms with the fact that there aren't always fairytale endings (or beginnings for that matter) and that any guarantee of happily ever after must begin with you.
Then a sense of serenity is born of acceptance.
So you begin making your way through the reality of today rather than holding out for the promise of tomorrow...
You realize that much of who you are and the way you navigate through life is, in great part, a result of all the social conditioning you've received over the course of a lifetime.

And you begin to sift through all the nonsense you were taught about :

- how you should look and how much you should weigh,
- what you should wear and where you should shop,
- where you should live or what type of car you should drive;
- who you should sleep with and how you should behave,
- who you should marry and why you should stay,
Slowly you begin to open up to new worlds and different points of view.

And you begin re-assessing and re-defining who you are and what you really believe in.

And you begin to discard the doctrines you have outgrown, or should never have practiced to begin with.
You accept the fact that you are not perfect, and that not everyone will love appreciate or approve of who or what you are... And that's OK... They are entitled to their own views and opinions. And, you come to terms with the fact that you will never be a size 8 or a perfect 10...
Or a perfect human being for that matter...

And you stop trying to compete with the image inside your head or agonizing over how you compare. And, you take a long look at yourself in the mirror and you make a promise to give yourself the same unconditional love and support you give so freely to others. Then a sense of confidence is born of self-approval.

And, you stop maneuvering through life merely as a consumer, hungry for your next fix, a new dress, another pair of shoes or looks of approval and admiration from family, friends or even strangers who pass by.
Then you discover that it is truly in giving that we receive, and that the joy and abundance you seek grows out of the giving.

And you recognize the importance of creating and contributing rather than obtaining and accumulating...
And you give thanks for the simple things you've been blessed with, things that millions of people upon the earth

can only dream about - a full refrigerator, clean running water, a soft warm bed, the freedom of choice and the opportunity to pursue your own dreams.

And you begin to love and to care for yourself.
You stop engaging in self-destructive behaviors, including participating in dysfunctional relationships.
You begin eating a balanced diet, drinking more water and exercising.

And because you've learned that fatigue drains the spirit and creates doubt and fear, you give yourself permission to rest.

And just as food is fuel for the body, laughter is fuel for the spirit and so you make it a point to create time for play.
Then you learn about love and relationships - how to love, how much to give in love, when to stop giving, and when to walk away.

You learn that people don't always say what they mean or mean what they say, intentionally or unintentionally, and that not everyone will always come through... And interestingly enough, it's not always about you.

So, you stop lashing out and pointing fingers or looking to place blame for the things that were done to you or weren't done for you.

And you learn to keep your Ego in check and to acknowledge and redirect the destructive emotions it spawns - anger, jealousy and resentment.
You learn how to forgive.......Quickly.......

You learn how to say I was wrong, and to forgive people for their own human frailties.

You learn to build bridges instead of walls and about the healing power of love as it is expressed through a kind word, a warm smile or a friendly gesture.

And, at the same time, you eliminate any relationships that are hurtful or fail to uplift and edify you.

You stop working so hard at smoothing things over and setting your needs aside.........

You learn that feelings of entitlement are perfectly OK and that it is your right to want or expect certain things.
And you learn the importance of communicating your needs with confidence and grace.

You learn that the only cross to bear is the one you choose to carry and that eventually martyrs are burned at the stake.

Then you learn to distinguish between guilt, and responsibility and the importance of setting boundaries and learning to say no...

You learn that you don't know all the answers, it's not your job to save the world and that sometimes you just need to Let Go.

Moreover, you learn to look at people as they really are and not as you would want them to be, and you are careful not to project your neediness or insecurities onto a relationship.

You learn that you will not be more beautiful, more intelligent, more lovable or important because of the man on your arm or the child that bears your name.
You learn that just as people grow and change, so it is with love and relationships, and that that not everyone can always love you the way you would want them to.
So you stop appraising your worth by the measure of, love you are given.

And suddenly you realize that it's wrong to demand that someone live their life or sacrifice their dreams just to serve your needs, ease your insecurities, or meet other peoples' standards and expectations. You learn that the only love worth giving and receiving is the love that is given freely without conditions or limitations.

And you learn what it means to love. So you stop trying to control people, situations and outcomes. You learn that alone does not mean lonely and you begin to discover the joy of spending time with yourself and on yourself... Then you discover the greatest and most fulfilling love you will ever know - Self Love.

And so it comes to pass that, through understanding, your heart heals; and now all new things are possible. Moving along, you begin to avoid toxic people and conversations. And you stop wasting time and energy rehashing your situation with family and friends. You learn that talk doesn't change things and that unrequited wishes can only serve to keep you trapped in the past.

So you stop lamenting over what could or should have been and you make a decision to leave the past behind. Then you begin to invest your time and energy to affect positive change.

You take a personal inventory of all your strengths and weaknesses and the areas you need to improve in order to move ahead, you set your goals and map out a plan of action to see things through. You learn that life isn't always fair and you don't always get what you think you deserve, and you stop personalizing every loss or disappointment.
You learn to accept that sometimes bad things happen to good people and that these things are not an act of God... But merely a random act of fate.

And you stop looking for guarantees, because you've learned that the only thing you can really count on is the unexpected and that whatever happens, you'll learn to deal with it. And you learn that the only thing you must truly fear is the great robber baron of all time - fear itself. So you learn to step right into and through your fears, because to give into fear is to give away the right to live life on your terms.

You learn that much of life truly is a self-fulfilling prophesy and you learn to go after what you want and not to squander your life living under a cloud of indecision or feelings of impending doom. Then you learn about money... The personal power and independence it brings and the options it creates. Slowly, you begin to take responsibility for yourself by yourself and you make yourself a promise to never betray yourself and to never ever settle for less than your hearts' desire.

And a sense of power is born of self-reliance. And you live with honor and integrity because you know that these principles are not the outdated ideals of a by-gone era but the mortar that holds together the foundation upon which you must build your life. And you make it a point to keep smiling, to keep trusting and to stay open to every wonderful opportunity and exciting possibility. Then you hang a wind chime outside your window to remind yourself what beauty there is in simplicity.

And finally...With courage in your heart and with God by your side you take a stand, you take a deep breath and you begin to design the life you want to live as best as you can.

So you sing like no one is listening,
You dance like no one is watching,
You work like you don't need the money,

And you love like you've never been hurt..."

Mistakes always precede the discovery of truth…….
"Difference is that raw and powerful connection from which our personal power is forged."

Fruit of the Spirit

The fruit of the Spirit is the outward indicator of salvation.
The fruit of the Spirit is living proof that the Spirit of God dwells in us.
The fruit of the Spirit is the supernatural outcome of being filled with the Holy Spirit.
The fruit of the Spirit id the result, manifestations, or expressions of the Holy Spirit through a believer's life;

Life Point: God loves us and wants us to love others through one another…….

Fruitful Step #1: Receive God's love by placing our faith in Jesus alone for salvation.

Fruitful Step #2: Be a launching pad for God's love by surrendering to the control of the Holy Spirit

The Higher You Climb

The higher you climb...The more that you see
The more that you see, the less that you know
The less that you know the more that you yearn
The more that you yearn...The higher you climb

The higher you climb the farther you reach ...The farther you reach The more that you touch...The more that you touch...The fuller you feel...The fuller you feel The less that you need...The less that you need...The higher you climb......................

Take Time

Take time to work, it is the price of success
Take time to think, it iws the source of power
Take time to play, it is the secret to perpetual youth
Take time to be friendly, it is the road to happiness
Take time to dream, it is expanding your horizons
Take time to love and be loved, it is a blessing from God
Take time to look around, the day is too short to be selfish
Take time to laugh, it is the music of the Soul.......

The Value Of Time Is The Value Of Life..................

How valuable is your time today?
How do you value each day?
How do you value each moment?
How do you value each minute?
How do you value each hour?

GOALS

G - Grab on to a dream.....
O - Offer to help others......
A - Acknowledge a plan
L - Leap for joy, be grateful
S - Service of giving............

Kindness is a virtue given by the Lord, it pays dividends in happiness and joy is it's reward. Proverbs 11:18, The wicked man earns deceptive wages, but he who sow righteousness reaps a sure reward...Today add kindness to someone else's life and your own happiness will be multiplied.

Proverbs 3:5-9, 28:7

MUSTARD SEED FAITH GROUP – (MSFG)

CODE OF ETHICS - COE

Integrity and ethics exist in the individual or they do not exist at all. They must be upheld by individuals or they are not up held at all. In order, for integrity and ethics to be characteristics of "The Mustard Seed Group," we who make up the "Group" must strive to be:

- Honest and trustworthy in all our relationships
- Reliable in carrying out task and responsibilities
- Truthful and accurate in what we say and do................
- Cooperate and constructive in all task and undertakings
- Fair and considerate in our treatment of all fellow

- **persons**
  - **Law abiding in all our activities………………………………..**
  - **Economical in utilizing all our resources…………………..**

Dedicated in services to ourselves and others to improvement of the quality of life in the world in which we live…..

Integrity and high standards of ethics require hard work, courage and difficult choices. Consultation between individuals will sometimes be necessary to determine a proper course of action. Integrity and ethics may sometimes require us to forgo other opportunities. In the long run, however, we will be better served by doing what is right rather than what is expedient……

"TEACH US TO NUMBER OUR DAYS"

TIME – MAKE THE MOST OF IT!

STRONG WOMAN vs WOMAN OF

STRENGTH

A strong woman works out every day to keep her body in shape but a woman of strength kneels in prayer to keep her soul in shape......................
A strong woman isn't afraid of anything but a woman of strength shows courage in the midst of her fear.......................
A strong woman won't let anyone get the best of her but a woman of strength gives the best of her to everyone............
A strong woman walks sure footedly but a woman of strength knows God will catch her when she falls.........................
A strong woman wears the look of confidence on her face but a woman of strength wears he grace..................................
A woman has faith that she is strong enough for the journey but a woman of strength has faith that it is in the journey that she will become strong.....................................

THE JOURNEY

Mistakes always precede the discovery of truth…

Do you think more than you know? Or…Do you know more than you think? What is Wisdom? Knowing the miracle….? Wisdom is not the same as knowledge and knowledge is not same as wisdom. There is no higher purpose in life than service to others. People are not the thoughts they think they are…Gathering information for the inside of yourself is finding the "Leader in You!" We are all living on borrowed time…. So use it wisely. Take out the trash in your mind. Take out what you don't need. The trash is anything that doesn't matter. Only then and only then…You can begin to maintain focus. Be………………… Conscientious ("Making an Arrival"), it is about choices we make and being responsible for our actions. Self-Interventions = Meaning + Purpose + Connection = Joy + Peace + Love within your purpose. Creating talent for living…Keeping in the present---Decide to Be Free! Diet + Exercise + Rest + Functional Faith = "YOU," "Healthy Concise Journey to living an adventurous tomorrow! It all starts Now! It all starts with You!! This is your adventures in a better, brighter future and it begins right here and right now!! So…. Fasten your seat belts for the ride of your life!!

Our days are like identical to suitcases, but some people pack more into them than others. That's because they know what to pack. Everybody gets twenty-four hours, but not everybody gets the same return on their twenty-four hours. The truth is, you don't manage your time, you manage your life. Time cannot be controlled; it marches on no matter what you do. Nobody – no matter how shrew – can save minutes. With all his wealth, Warren Buffett can't buy additional hours for his day. People talk about trying to "find time," but they need to quit looking; there isn't any extra lying around. Twenty-four hours is the best any of us is going to get. Wise people understand that time is their most precious commodity. As a result, they know where their time goes. They continually analyze how they are using their time and ask themselves, "Am I getting the best use out of my time? In his book "What To Do Between Birth and Death," " The Art of Growing UP," Charles Spezzano writes: " You don't really pay for things with money, you pay for them with time, We say 'In five years, I'll have enough money put away for that vacation house we want. Then I'll slow down.' That means the house will cost you five years – one-twelfth of your adult life. Translate the dollar value of the house, car, or anything else into time, and then see if it's still worth it,"

"ABOUT COMMITMENTS"

When you measure your life by the yardstick, you've a better chance of living by the right commitments. There are three type of commitments: (1) Dramatic commitments. Like getting married or buying a home. Unfortunately, we don't consider the hidden costs. When we buy a house we think only of the additional square footage, not the extra hour each day commuting to work or the time taken away from our family. (2) Routine commitments. (3) Unspoken commitments. These are the commitments we make to ourselves, but often fail to keep. In life, the dramatic commitments receive most of our attentions, but the routine ones end up controlling us. Because there are so many of them and because they come on a daily basis and individually look so small, we don't sense the gap growing between what we say matters most to us, and what we're actually doing with our lives....So let's simplify it: "Love the Lord....and...Love your neighbor............"Amen"

"ABOUT MISTAKES"

Learn from your mistakes, correct the ones you can, and continue being decisive. Don't fall back into a pattern of indecision because you got it wrong a few times. Devote a reasonable amount of time to waiting on God, and when necessary seek the counsel of others. But don't be afraid to act; make a decision and follow through with it. In other words,

> *"JUST DO IT!"*
>
> *(1) Admit your mistakes*
> *(2) Accept mistakes as the price of progress*
> *(3) Insist on learning from your mistakes..........*
> *"Mistakes always precede the discovery of truth!"*

POSITIVE THOUGHTS

F U T U R E - Faithful Understanding Together with Useful Rich Excellence

P O W E R - Purpose – Opportunity – Wisdom - Excellence - Respect

T R U Teenage Racial Understanding "Difference is that raw and powerful connection from which our personal power is forged."

A B C Amazing Blessings Campaign, means Humanity!

AMAZING …A =ABILITIES M =MEANINGFUL A =AFFECTIVELY Z =ZESTFUL I =INSPIRATIONAL N =NICE G =GRACIOUSLY

BLESSINGS … B =BEING L =LOYALTY E =EFFECTIVE S =SOCIETY S =SAVING I =INTERNATIONAL N =NECESSARY G =GAINFUL S =SEEDS

CAMPAIGN C =CONTINUE A =ADMIRATION M =MORE P = PEOPLE A =ACTION I =INTEREST G =GOOD..N =NEEDFULLY

Earth Angels

*Feel the presence of Angels as you walk among friends,
For each one serves a purpose and on them we do depend.
They console and encourage us when troubles seem to unfold. Their strength helps to carry us when we need to be strong and bold.
We might not see their wings; yet they're always near to share our happiness and our sorrows, and we know how much they care. We call them our "Earth Angels" that are sent from God above to share our earthly journey and to fill us with their love.............*

A Healthy Soul!!!

Choose to be Happy Every Moment!!!

Try closing your eyes now. When you close your eyes, you can focus on yourself. And then give yourself a a big hug! "You did a really good job today!"

The sun floating in the sky!

They sky embracing the sun!

A human mind as wide as the sky, passionate as the sun, living in the world; Like nature, people create their own world; The sun shining like a jewel, the moon becoming dim the wind bringing fresh energy and from time to time, the falling rain, helping to make life stand stronger! There is nothing that isn't part of something. At the last moment, warm human eyes watching everything....as nature makes the flower buds burst, waiting for spring in full bloom...When you accept the gift of a spring bouquet of positive, you will hear bells of gratitude as you are also, part of nature's action of spring in full bloom..........

Some Food For Your Healthy Soul!

Just like the importance of choosing nutritious food for the health of your body and mind. You are then……..physically and mentally, does this mean you are really healthy? One more aspect of health to consider is the health of the soul, or spiritual health. What does it mean to have a healthy soul or to be spiritually healthy? It means that having positive values strengthens the soul. It means that we have to be carefully about the kinds of thoughts we invite in. So, what can we do to make our soul healthy? Our soul need good nutrition just like the body does. The soul that consumes hate becomes exhausted, while the soul that consumes love becomes enriched. The quality of our thoughts determines the quality of our life. When the soul harbors loving thoughts, the soul becomes healthier. What do you do in your free time? Do you sit staring blankly watching the world go by, or do you smile laugh or cry? Do you neglect your soul and leave it to be fed by negative information from the world? Your soul has muscles too. Information that makes you passive and has no nutritional value renders your soul powerless. Good thoughts are needed to make your soul strong and healthy.

So how can we exercise good thoughts? It's not that difficult. Try writing or thinking one line of positive words a day, while looking into your soul. When your soul aches or when you feel empty, just start to write or think good and positive things. Plant trees in the forest of your soul, water them, remove the weeds or bad things around them, when the sun shines, your soul will brighten and grow. Then one day your soul, having become greater and deeper, will shine too! If your soul becomes healthier, you can come to know yourself as you really are meant to be. You can see thinks about yourself that you did not know, did not want to know, or pretended not to know. If you come to know yourself, you can see yourself as the beauty shines within. You will see the kind and caring person that you did not acknowledge emerging in full bloom. You will see clearly, if you come to know your true inner self. You will believe in the value and strength and have courage to live in harmony with others. This will allow, YOU, to grow together with others. Reading the writing of someone else's soul can be a stepping stone to the growth of your own soul.

This is just a modest meal, the food to your soul, will

be more than satisfying for you. What's more is the sincere hope that you will and can become someone who abundantly serves others food for the soul. Are you truly ready? Is your soul ready?

The Power Of The Positive - A world where we receive applause, where we all cheer with hope and breathe with optimism!

Fortunately, there is a magic potion that makes our ordinary lives special and enriched. It is having the insight to see the same thing in a different way - to be positive. When you want to give up, when things are so difficult that you cannot cope, try taking a deep, deep breath.....try taking a stroll through a beautiful green forest in your mind. Eventually, breathing, like hope, will enable you to keep going. Before you know it, the growing power of the positive will help you create dreams for the future and having these dreams will bring you happiness. Try closing your eyes now. When you close your eyes, you can focus on yourself. Say to yourself sincerely, "I give thanks to the heavens, I give thanks to humanity and I give thanks to mother earth, and then give, yourself a big hug. Don't live according to others' standards, waiting to receive applause. Give yourself your own applause also, don't forget, to applaud others no matter what! Become a flower blooming in the desert! Always stride to do your best no matter what! Even if it is something small, your great soul will continue to grow pure. Give praise and give applause. What about the sun that rose again today? Rather than being lazy, the sun rose again to make us warm. Isn't this enough to deserve applause and give thanks?

Expressing gratitude and appreciation shouldn't be difficult. Nor should it be something saved for special occasions. All life is worthy of applause simply because it exists. Why don't we change the tendency in our society to only give applause for exceptional abilities or excellence? Why don't we try creating a world in which everyone can receive applause? Let's give ourselves, our family, our friends, and our colleagues, applause. Then, when we feel worn out and tired, at least we won't feel alone because someone will be cheering over our shoulder. Finding small miracles in everyday life and believing, my soul is positive and the happiness of wisdom.

Our face is a smile VOX. Not a box with a smiley face on it, but a box containing something which makes others smile too! There are two good ways to make your face bright. These are none other than positive thinking and smiling. This is no other than a miracle of life, bringing hope will be able to create miracles in everyday life. Just act positive! If you act positive, you will become positive. Breathe hope! Hope comes in, desperations goes out. If you breathe hope, you don't need to call for it desperately. If you breathe hope you don't need to feel afraid. Breathe hope!

They Will Soar On Wings Like Eagles. (Isaiah 40:31)

God's Promise To Us Is...................Strength

The Lord is my light and my salvation; whom shall I fear? (Psalm 27:1) The Lord is the strength of my life; of who shall I be afraid? I will strengthen thee; yea, I will help thee; yea, I will uphold thee with the right hand of my righteousness. (Isaiah 41:10

Spiritual Blindness

Just because you cannot see it, doesn't mean

it does not exist.............What does it mean to see with spiritual eyes? God exist through the spiritual eyes of man and nature....a touch, a smile, the wind, the rain, snow, sun, the moon, the stars; all are God's way of reminding us to not live in spiritual blindness. We exist because...He, exist...we are His creation...He is our creator; all is because...He Is..................

UC - UNIVERSIAL CONNECTIVITY...

We cannot grasp formless, of the oneness we are seeing, emptiness is the inner nature Within the outer form of being.......Life is a Journey not a destination continuing forwarding pathways into stages...into Phase...into a very valued, journey....As water has been primary to the life of the earth, UC - Universal Connectivity has been fundamental to spiritual vitality of the world. UC, inspires us to awaken a deeper feeling about life; It touches the hearts of humankind everywhere to bestow upon with the universe......................

Novices often have little understanding of the multi-faceted history and complex evolution of the laws that govern the universe. It continues to flow on its journey to many of cultures over the centuries.

UC can be expressed and enhanced through everyday life, in work and play, in art and sports; it transforms the mundane into the sublime, the temporal into the eternal. The human mind becomes one with its inner spirit, refreshed with the waters of UC.

UC's journey around the world present a history, but as a spiritual odyssey. Gathered together is the entire pathway, stages and phases of UC. The jouney unfolds before you as a spiritual companion traveling across time and space, circling the globe. There's intellectual foundation for understanding UC's passage around the world, which offers us help to gain a clearer foundation of what is so relevant to us all.   UC points directly to the spirit that shines like a beacon in the night to show us the Way into these pathways, stages, and phases into a very valued universal journey............... the developmental embraces, diversity and even conflict; yet through it all, the spirit of UC is always present. Spiritual interaction between to be; is transmitted to help create the enlightenment of practical interaction within oneness, coming from something wonderful with a higher consciousness. Spiritual practice of meditation is the discovery of a long- established advance awakening, a disciplined method of focusing attention and clearing the mind to achieve union with the universe.

The theory is toward true nature and harmony that encompasses everything. The entire thrust of contending a universal, spiritual principle that we are all a part of and yet lies beyond us; seeking to yield to an experience of unity with inspiration and guidance. The source of meaning is the spiritual way of things, united to gain wisdom through the word of "God," sensitivity and insight. This brings about the union of seeking balance, to include both sides to be unified in the wholeness within a pathway to allow the natural course of events to take place. The order of acquiring knowledge, in becoming one with an order of happiness, fulfillment, and true wisdom of humanity is inherently, an expression of giving balance to a fuller, tranquil conception of peace within; allowing permeated structured renunciation of a positive view of humanity, and harmony with the universal law of "God" that governs our "Way," joined with the path to truth, to reaching understanding ....as the light of dawning into for a profound horizon.

The essence to achieve direct powerful force emerging fertile developmental flowering, influences inspiration that touches a reawaking, rekindling to flourishing a deep spiritual understanding of our own true nature; This is the beginning roots to an ultimate existence of one's inner nature. This is an emerging demonstration of a logical link equivalent to conception and co-exiting with the fulfillment of fullness which is the opposition of emptiness. It is defined by virtue of contrast parts of component parts bolted together in synthesis. As an analogy compounded together, through inter-relationship, to exist as a unity and being codependent. Existing only through contrast to the other, threads within the tapestry releasing the ascetic achievement of the transitory means to peaceful conceptualized of legitimate comprehensible growth; to a developed management of a devoted functional positive statement to a clear lifestyle management supported by, to and for passages giving us pathways, stages and phases into…a very valuable journey……………It begins **WITH, COLORS OF THE RAINBOW AND BEYOND……**

The rainbow is not located at a specific distance, but from a certain angle. Thus, a rainbow is not an object, and cannot be physically approached. Indeed, it is impossible for an observer to see a rainbow from any angle other than the customary one of 42 degrees from the directional opposite. Even if an observer sees another observer who seems "under" or "at the end of" a rainbow, the second observer will see a different rainbow—further off—at the same angle as seen by the first observer. A rainbow spans a continuous spectrum of colors. Any distinct bands perceived are an artifact of human colour vision, and no banding of any type is seen in a black-and-white photo of a rainbow, only a smooth gradation of intensity to a maximum, then fading towards the other side. For colors seen by the human eye, the most commonly cited and remembered sequence is sevenfold red, orange, yellow, green, blue, indigo/violet.

The colors of the rainbow are fresh, vibrant, cheerful and amazingly deep. Seeing a rainbow can easily improve the mood of all people, making them feel better and happier. The seven colors of the rainbow emanate; Primary colors red, yellow and blue. From these colors emanate orange, green, indigo and violet.

Rainbow Colors and Their Meaning...................

1. Blue

Blue is one of the most powerful colors of the rainbow. This is the color of distance, oceans, skies, but also the color of the heaven. Blue has always been considered a color of energy, expanding perceptions to the unknown. Blue is also thought to be the color of divinity. This color is able to bring peace and understanding, calm and relaxation. The color also enhances communication and offers a feeling of peace and happiness. It expresses spirituality............

2. Yellow

Yellow is the color of the sun. It expresses energy and life. This color brings clarity of thought, orderliness, memory improvement, but it is also able to alleviate confusion and improve decision making skills. This is the color of wisdom......................................

3. Red

Red has always been considered the color of passion. This is the color of activity, too. Red sustains physical body movement, brings energy, enthusiasm, but also passion and security. Red stands for vitality…………………

4. Orange

Orange combines two colors: red and yellow, so it includes both energy and wisdom. Orange is considered to be a color of dynamic energy, bringing creativity, playfulness, relief from boredom and equilibrium……………………………

5. Green

Green has always been the color of life. The human eye is able to recognize more variations of green than in any other color. This color expresses harmony, health, balance, abundance, but also sympathy and growth………

6. Indigo

Indigo is believed to amplify energy in a more profound way than blue. It expresses wisdom, sudden awareness, intuition and psychic abilities……………………………………..

7. Violet

Violet is considered to be the ray of the spiritual mastery. Violet is formed by a combination of red and blue. It brings energy and it is associated with spiritual attainment and healing………………………….

****
****

Having under consideration the effects that colors can have on individuals, there is no wonder that the rainbow can make everyone happier. Actually, a rainbow is considered to be a unique impressive spectacle of the nature

==There some interesting things about rainbows:==

1. Every time we see a rainbow, it's after the rain. It means that the sun is always

behind you and the rain in front of you when a rainbow appears. Thus, the center of the rainbow's arc is directly opposite the sun.

2. **Many believe that the colors of the rainbow are only red, orange, yellow, green, blue & indigo but a rainbow is formed from numerous colors, even from those we can't see.**

3. **People can see the colors of a rainbow due to the light of various colors that is refracted when goes from one medium, such as air, and into another, in our case, the raindrops formed up from water.**

4. **Every one of us sees their own "personal" rainbow. When you look at a rainbow, for example, you see the lights reflected of certain raindrops, while the person next to you, looking at the same rainbow, may see the light reflecting from a different angle, so it's different. It means that every person sees rainbow colors accordingly to light and how her eyes perceive it.**

4. The end of a rainbow can never be reached. When you move, the rainbow that you see with your eyes, moves as well as the raindrops are found in various sports in the atmosphere. In a few words, the rainbow will always move while you are moving, at the same rate. People happier and actually everyone is happy when seeing a rainbow*****************
****

SPIRITUAL COLORS OF OUR RAINBOW & BEYOND......ATTITUDE/PERSPECTIVE/PASSION/ POWER/POISE********************************
****
****

A T T I T U D E: The longer you live, the more you will realize the impact of attitude on life...Attitude is more important than facts. It is more important than appearance, gifts or skills. It will make or break a company, a church, a home, and/or a, marriage. The remarkable thing is that we have a choice everyday regarding the attitude we will embrace for that day. We cannot change our past...we cannot change the fact that people will act in a certain way. We cannot change the inevitable. Life is 10% what happens to us and 90% how we react to it.....and so "YOU," are in charge of your attitude, which determines your altitude in life......A T T I T U D E   I S   Y O U.....reaching your altitude potential........

P E R S P E C T I V E: Extending to a distance; a vista. The manner in which objects appear in respect to their relative position in one's mental view, fact and/or ideas and their interrelationships.............The ability to see all the relevant data in meaningful relationship............P E R S P E C T I V E I S S P I R I T U A L   A B I L I T I E S........................

P A S S I O N: A compelling strong amorous feeling.....Love, desire, fondness, enthusiasm or for something. The object of passion, an outburst of.....P A S S I O N I S......W I T H I N.

P O W E R: Ability, to do or act of doing or

accomplishing something...The capability marked by the ability to act. The possession of command authority to influence.... Ascendancy position of great forceful spiritual strength....................==SPIRITUAL COLORS OF OUR RAINBOW & BEYOND==........................

P O I S E: A state of balance or equilibrium, as from equality or equal distribution...A dignified self-confident manner, bearing, composure of......Steadiness, stability of the way of being poised, held or carried...The state of positioning to adjust or carry in equilibrium balance evenly........==P O W E R o f P O I S E== is balance in action.........balancing our rainbow and beyond ***********************************
****
****
****
****
****

WALKING A

GODLY LIFE

Just think......you're here not by chance, but by God's choosing. His hand formed you and made you the person you are.
He compares you to no one else---you are one of a kind. You lake nothing that His grace can't give you;
He has allowed you to be here at this time in history to fulfill His special purpose for this generation.
You are God's servant in God's place at God's perfect time.
He has given us His very great and precious promises, so that through them you may participate in the divine nature.
II Peter 1:4

<u>Do you think more than you know? Or.....Do you know more than you think? What is Wisdom??? Knowing the miracle........????Wisdom is not the same as knowledge and knowledge is not same as wisdom. There is no higher purpose in life than service to others. People are not the thoughts they think they are.....Gathering information for the inside of yourself is finding the "Faith in You!" We are all living on borrowed time....so use it wisely. Take out the trash in your mind.</u>

*<u>Do not be anxious about anything, but in everything, by prayer and petition with thanksgiving, present your requests to God.
Phil 4:6</u>*

*Excess Baggage Weighing You Down ? ? ?
What is your baggage from the past labeled?*

Is it "Un-forgiveness/Anger?"- Be kind compassionate to

one another, forgiving each other, just as in Christ God forgave you!
Ephesians 4:32

DEFINITIONS OF UNFORGIVENESS/ANGER STYLES

1. Avoidance
2. Sneaky
3. Paranoid
4. Explosive
5. Shameful
6. Deliberate
7. Addictive
8. Habitual
9. Moral
10. Hate

<u>Then Jesus said, "Come to Me, all of you who are weary and carry heavy burdens, and I will give you rest. Take my yoke upon you. Let me teach you, because I am humble and gentle, and you will find rest for your souls. For my yoke fits perfectly, and the burden I give you is light." - Matthew 11:28 - 30</u>

<u>1. Consciously decide to choose a "GODLY" life.</u>
<u>2. Seek God First!</u>

First
Rely
On
God

2. Get close to Jesus! Develop one now through: (prayer, bible study and small group).
3. Get into action now, ask for help! - Courage is standing on the inside out..........

<u>GOD IS IN CONTROL! ! !</u>

I can do everything through Him who gives me strength. - Phil 4:13

He who began a good work in you will be faithful to complete it. - Phil 1:6

Characteristics of a Godly Individual Overcoming Adversity

Refinement - (Sin - Surrender - Repentance) - Attention
John 16:33, Adversity

The Book of Job

Chapter 1

Verses 1-5 (Introduction) Spiritually mature with wisdom, measure spiritually uprightness; Verses 6-22 (Testing) Upholding faith maturity……………..

Chapter 2

(Loyalty) - Continue to praise him through the adversity...

Chapter 3

(Compassion) - Inspiration and encouragement through comfort

Chapter 4

(Transformation) - Friendship in adversity

Chapter 5

(Correction) - Building character

Divine Diagnosis

The Sovereignty of God!

Knowing God better is accomplishing God's will . . .(Refinement)

Understanding purposeful determination through the measurse of his foundation is the cornerstone,

Matthew 6:26 - Look at the birds of the sky; they don't sow or reap or gather into barns, yet your heavenly Father feeds then. Aren't you worth more than they? ? ?

They Will Soar On Wings Like Eagles. (Isaiah 40:31)

God's Promise To Us Is...................Strength

The Lord is my light and my salvation; whom shall I fear? (Psalm 27:1) The Lord is the strength of my life; of who shall I be afraid? I will strengthen thee; yea, aI will help thee; yea, I will uphold thee with the right hand of my righteousness. (Isaiah 41:10

SPIRITUAL RISK MANAGEMENT ENRICHMENT PROCESS

STEP 1 - COLLECT DATA AND INFORMATION - The systematic collection of data used to comprehend the risk universe, gain a historical perspective of the identified risk, and establish a baseline risk.

STEP 2 - ANALYZE AND ASSESS RISK - Use of analytical tools to determine the areas of greatest risk, and scope of the problem in those areas.

STEP 3 - PRESCRIBE ACTION - Design a course of action and assign appropriate resources to address the determined risk.

STEP 4 - TRACK AND REPORT - Results are complied, and reported back into the "Risk Management Process" for monitoring of future action.

GIVING "HIM" - HONOR, PRAISE & THANKS . . . . ALWAYS ! ! ! !

........SPIRITUAL HAPPINESS IS NOT A DESTINATION........IT IS A METHOD OF LIFE............

Spirit Soul Connection - Dr. Rhonda Dula,
http://www.starnow.com/RhondaDula
http://www.facebook.com/rhonda.dula
E-Mail Address: dularhonda@gmail.com

"Once Upon A Midnight

Clear,"

"Is to know that, God is with us in everything we do!" Proverbs 4: 25-27
Let your eyes look straight ahead, and your eyelids look before you. Ponder the path of your feet, and let all your ways be established. Do not turn to the right or the left.

The Purpose

Regardless of our religious background, we need to know how the three purposes of solving our three greatest needs. Understanding God's gifts transforms lives….forever! God's gift to us has three qualities that make it unique. First, it is the most expensive gift we'll ever receive. It's priceless. Jesus paid for it with his life. Second, it's the only gift we'll ever receive that will last forever. Finally, it is an extremely practical gift---one we'll use every day for the rest of our lives……..

1.) A time for celebration. This is the day of the Lord's victory; let us be happy, let us celebrate! Psalm 118:24

2.) A time for salvation. When the right time finally came, God sent his own Son. He came as the son of a human mother and lived under the Jewish Law. Galatians 4:4

3). A time for reconciliation. Now we rejoice in our wonderful new relationship with God---all because what our Lord Jesus Christ has done…making us friends of God. Romans 5:11

4). It's important to bring gratitude to the forefront of our daily---not just during a special holiday, but all year long. But living a life of gratitude is a choice. Life doesn't have to be perfect in order for us to give—we can choose to be grateful, regardless of our challenging circumstances. It pleases the Lord when we have an "attitude of gratitude."

A Letter from HIM………………

My name is God. You hardly have time for me.
I love you and always bless you. I am always with you
I need you to spend 10% of your 24 hours with Me today.
Just praise and pray.

We must go through the storm to appreciate the sunshine!
Be The Change! *********Make a difference today.

2 Cor.12:9

(FI) - FELLOWSHIP INTERNATIONAL

Affirms the Lordship of Christ over all aspects of life, acknowledges the Bible as the foundational authority for the development of committed to high goals and clarifies the implications of biblical truth for its discipline. By developing servant leaders who value integrity, compassion, and justice in all aspects of Christian life, prepares individuals to serve, not to be served.

23 Psalm - For The Christian Business and Work Place:

The Lord is my real boss, and I shall not want.
He gives me peace, when chaos is all around me.
He gently reminds me to pray before I speak and to do all things without complaining.

He reminds me that He is my Source and not my job. He restores my sanity every day and guides my decisions that I might honor Him in everything I do.

Even though, I face absurd amounts of unrealistic deadlines, budget cutbacks, and aging body that doesn't cooperate every day. I will not stop- for He is with me! His presence, His peace and His power will see me through.

He raises me up even when others do not.
He claims me as His own, even when things seem dark.
His faithfulness and love is always better!
When it's all said and done, I'll be working for Him a whole lot longer and for that, I bless His name........

THE GOVERNMENT OF GOD

1. Minister of finance 💰 Haggai 2:8 Silver & gold are mine.

2. Minster of Education 📚 Hosea 4:6 My people perish because of lack of knowledge.

3. Minister of Roads 🏃 John 14:6 I am the way, the truth & life. No one comes to my Father except through me"

4. Minister of Tourism 🚗🚌 us Mark 16:15 Go into all corners of the world & preach good news to every creature

5. Minister of Labor 💼💻🔧 Matt 9:37 Harvest is abundant but workers are few

6. Minister of Sports - Matthew 19:30 Many who are first will be last & many who are last will be first. Corinthians 9:24, 27 🏁 Be like athlete, run so that you will be the first.

7. Minister of Transportation ✈ Matthew 11:28 Come to me, all who are tired from carrying heavy loads & I will give you rest

8. Minister of Health 🩹💉♣ Isaiah 53:5 He took our infirmities, we are healed

9. Minister of Internal Security 🔪🔫💣 Isaiah 54:17 No weapon formed against me shall prosper

10. Minister of Agriculture 🌱🍃🌿 John 15:1 I am the true vine & my Father is the gardener. He cuts off every branch in me that bears no fruits

11. Minister of Faith (Hebrews 11:1; Hebrews 6:17; Ephesians 2:8-9)

Spirit Soul Connection - Dr. Rhonda Dula, http://www.starnow.com/RhondaDula http://www.facebook.com/rhonda.dula

"Once Upon A Midnight Clear"

****

TAKE TIME -

Take time to work - it is the price of success..

Take time to think - it is the source of power.....

Take time to play - it is the secret to perpetual youth.....

Take time to be friendly - it is the road to happiness.....

Take time to dream it is expanding your horizons.....

Take time to love and be loved - it is a blessing from God.....

Take time to look around - the day is too short to be selfish.....

Take time to laugh - it is the music of the soul..

- **THE HIGHER YOU CLIMB** -

The higher you climb ....

　　　　　　　　　　　The more you see.....

　　　　　　　　　　　The more you see - the less that you know.....

　　　　　　　　　　　The less that you know - the more that you yearn.....

　　　　　　　　　　　The more that you yearn - the higher you climb.....

　　　　　　　　　　　The higher you climb - the farther you reach.....

　　　　　　　　　　　The farther you reach - the more that you touch.....

　　　　　　　　　　　The more that you touch - the fuller you feel.....

　　　　　　　　　　　The fuller you feel - the

less that you need.....

 The less that you need –
The higher you climb…………………………………

A C T S

A DORATION
C ONFESSION
T HANKSGIVING
S UPPLICATIONS

ADORATION – God alone is worth of our adoration and praise. This is time to focus on His greatness, majesty, and love for us. Spend time praising the Lord and adoring Him for who He is (Matthew 6:9). Use Scripture to praise Him (Psalm 103, 145, 150; Revelation 4:8, 5:12-14)……………………………………………

CONFESSION – Confession allows us to clear away the sins that harm's us and our relationship with God. Sin is destructive relationships and our own lives. In our Spend time asking Jesus to search our heart for sin in our life (Psalm 139:23-24), confessing and repenting of (turning away from) sins and accept His forgiveness and cleansing (1 John 1:8-9)……………………………………

THANKSGIVING – God blesses us constantly. Take time to recall the wonderful things that God has done and the gifts we have been given. Give thanks for all His blessings, people, and guidance (Philippians 4:6-7). Give thanks for His salvation through Jesus Christ (Psalm 118:P21, Acts 4:12). Thank Him for His goodness, loving-kindness, and faithfulness (Psalm 100:4-6).

SUPPLICATION – Ask God for our needs and the needs of others. This is supplication, or intercession; as believers in prayer (Luke 18:1; Colossians 4:2; 1 Timothy 2:1-4)……………..Intercessory Prayer…………………..
Pray for healing, recovery, the church, countries, missionaries, governments, (Acts 12:5; Romans 10:1; Matthew 6:11-13). Pray for world issues; for the Gospel to be preached, for leaders and those in influential positions, for the persecuted church, justice for the poor and relief of suffering. Jesus encourages us to do so in the Lord's Prayer – He gave us the model for prayer, (Matthew 6:9-13)…………

CODE OF ETHICS - (COE)

"Difference is that raw and powerful connection from which our personal power is forged."

Integrity and ethics exist in the individual or they do not exist at all. They must be upheld by individuals or they are not up held at all………….. In order, for integrity and ethics to be within our characteristics we must strive to be:

- **Honest and trustworthy in all our relationships**
-
- Reliable in carrying out task and responsibilities
-
- **Truthful and accurate in what we say & do……**

-
  - Cooperate & constructive in all task & undertakings
-
  - Fair/considerate in our treatment of all fellow persons
-
  - Economical in utilizing all our resources…………

    Dedicated in services to ourselves and others to improve the quality of life in the world in which we live…………………..

Integrity and high standards of ethics require hard work, courage and major choices. Consultation between individuals will be necessary to determine a proper course of action. Integrity and ethics may sometimes require us to sacrifice our own individual opportunities. In the long run, however, we will be better served by doing what is right rather than what is expedient. . . . .

TRAINING

GODS PURSUES A *LOVING* RELATIONSHIP WITH US………………

- ***God Tells Us:***

    - In "James 1" that we are to face trials with joy……………………

- "James 1:4" Tells us that perseverance must finish its work so that we may be mature and complete, not lacking anything....................

==GODS WANTS US TO <u>JOIN HIM</u> IN THE MINISTRY OF RECONCILIATION.................==

- <u>*Love Leads to Reconciliation:*</u>

- God continues to reach out to us through scripture, teaching us "He" has done what it takes for us to be reconciled with "Him."

- We are now "His" ambassadors, helping others experience reconciliation with "God" the same we have; letting "God" show them "His" love through us............................

- <u>*Final, Total, and Complete:*</u>
- No matter what the circumstances are, "God's" love never changes.

- God takes the initiative to bring us into a deeply personal relationship with "Him."

- **_Sharing with Others God's Love Never Changes:_**
  - God wants us to view each other as partners in ministry. Pray that "God" will make us committed and effective disciple makers…………………………………………………

GOD SAYS………..IT IS OUR PURPOSE……………

GOD LEADS US TO _CRISIS_ OF BELIEF……………

- **_Walking By Faith_**
- **_God Puts Confidence in Our Heart_**
- **_Put Faith into Action_**

- A faithful servant is one who does what the "Master" tells them, whatever the outcome may be. Consider…….. "JESUS" ……..He endured the cross, but now He is seated next to the throne God! What a reward for faithfulness! Let us not grow weary in being faithful……….Our reward(s) awaits!

JESUS IS LORD - HIS WORD IS SUPREME

"The Seven Principals"

1). Unity
2). Self-determination
3). Collective work and responsibility
4). Cooperative economics
5). Purpose
6). Creativity
7). Faith

A "body," standing tall is a bold and beautiful way to greet the world. Good posture says as much about your state of mind as it does your physical condition. When your skeleton is correctly aligned, your body is at its most efficient. You absorb and distribute force from movement without overstressing your joints, your muscles are arrayed at just the right length and tension, allowing your brain to communicate with them at optimal speed. Plus, you're poised to meet the world. Standing tall--with a lifted, open chest, relaxed shoulders and a lengthened neck--conveys confidence and vitality. Good body posture is a brave stance, because you're exposing a strong heart, what a bold and beautiful way to greet the world! But you can't simply will yourself into proper alignment. Bad habits, a sedentary lifestyle and muscular misuse can cause postural deviations. If not corrected, they can result in muscular imbalances, pain, even injury. One common postural misalignment pattern is upper-cross syndrome, characterized by rounded shoulders and the head jutting forward. It often occurs among people who sit a great deal. Suffers experience back pain, burning between the shoulder blades, neck stiffness, lack of energy (especially after long hours working at the computer) and headaches that are worse at the end of the workday. Fixing upper-crossed syndrome is a 2 part process:

1). "Stretching," chest and neck muscles that might be

tight and restricting movement.

2). "Strengthening," muscles in the shoulder regions that are weak and unstable. Good postures take practice, but don't be surprise if you find yourself feeling as confident and openhearted as you look!

==Freestyle Movement II - Your Personal Training ! !==

==Stretching and Strengthening Freestyle Movements:==

==The Stretching Movements:==

Chest Stretch - Stand next to a wall, with your right shoulder facing it and your hips pointing straight ahead; bend your right elbow to 90 degrees and rest your elbow, forearm and side of hand against the wall at shoulder height. Your palm should face forward; your upper arm should be parallel to the floor. Take one large step forward with your left leg, keeping your elbow in place. You should feel a stretch through your chest and in front of your shoulder. Rotate your torso and hips slightly to your left to deepen the stretch. Hold 20-30 seconds. Repeat on the opposite side. Hold your elbow slightly higher than your shoulder to feel the stretch more in the upper chest. Drop your elbow lower than your shoulders to stretch your Pecs. Do 10-15 repetitions per right side stretch and 10-15 repetitions per left side stretch.

Cervical Stretch - Sit on a stool, stability ball or straight-backed chair; Keep your shoulders lowered and pulled back and draw in your belly button toward your spine. Bend your left arm and put it behind your back. Hold each stretch for 20-30 seconds. Keeping your head straight, bring your right ear toward your right shoulder. You'll feel a stretch on the left side of your neck. Repeat, when you feel the stretch, turn your gaze to the ceiling over your left ear and your chin should rotate a little further up; to the left than it did in the previous stretch. Repeat stretch and lower your chin toward your left shoulder. You should feel a stretch behind your neck on the left side. Repeat the entire sequence with your right arm behind your back, bringing your left ear toward your left shoulder. Repeat the entire sequence with both the right/left side 10-15 repetitions....

The Strengthening Movements:

The Seagull - Strengthens the muscles that stabilize and control the upper back. You'll need to a set of dumb or something similar. Lie on your stomach on a bed, weight bench table. Dangle your head and arms over the edge, which should come right under your armpits. Relax your neck and let your head drop. Hold the weights with your palms facing your thumbs pointing forward. When you look down, the weights should be in line with your nose. Bend your elbows to 90 degrees. Lift bent elbows toward the ceiling as far as you can go. Hold for a moment, then, slowly lower. Do 10 to 15 reps, rest briefly, and repeat twice more.........

Stick 'Em Up - Strengthen your back and stretches your chest muscles. Sit against a wall, legs crossed or bent. Press the back of your head and all of your vertebrae into the wall. Raise your elbows, bent at 90 degrees, to shoulder height. Rest the backs of your hands and wrists against the wall. Keeping your back to the wall, slide your hands up the wall, slowly straightening your elbows. Stop when you can no longer maintain your alignment. Lower your elbows against the wall. Do three sets, of 10 to 15 reps each......

......S   u   c   C   E   S   S.......

Seeking...Utilization...Communication...Community...Expression...Spirit...Security........

Seeking the Truth

Utilization of Creative Talent

Communication and Commitment

Community and Service

Expression and Self-Confidence

Spirit of Belief

Security Assessment and Management

****

s u c c e s s

Life's hectic......That's a given......But the daily drill doesn't have to get the better of you.....That's were "Smart & Simple" comes in. Because sometimes the best answers are the simple ones.....Sometimes the path to feeling great from head to toe, from morning to night, is simpler than you might imagine.....It's about small changes that are good for you.....It's about lifestyle choices that make a real difference in your success..... It's about living life..... "Smart....And Simple"..... Balanced Living.....Visualize a Healthier You.....Eat Better and Live Better.....Get Stronger.....Feel Stronger.... Increase Your Memory.....Imagine Yourself Enjoying a Better Life Style......Guided imagery harness the power of imagination to induce relaxation and reduce stress....In a nutshell, you focus intently on ...S U C

C E S S ......For instance, if you see yourself in your mind's eye walking in SUCCESS step by step......SUCCESS becomes Your Life Style Guided imagery is one of a group of mind-body techniques that focus on the interaction between mental and physical factors as they influence overall health and well-being.....An underlying assumption of these techniques is that people with a variety of positive energy can play an active role in managing their lifestyle ......Guide imagery is a learned and practiced technique.....Imagery training is also a qualified approach in enhancing social activities and the emotional support needed to improve your well-being.....which promotes your "Life Style. . . . .

The stepping stone to Security Assessment of your future has given you a new hope through Healthy Balance, Life Style Management, Development and Foundation. These are all the tools you will need to create a purposeful objective added with motivation of your newly discovered leadership qualities. You've been given inspiration, direction, instruction and guidelines. Now it is time for you to put those puzzle pieces together. Creating and Selecting a Life Management Theme means: Asking the Right Questions to Get the Right Answer - Now Put Your Puzzle Pieces Together!!

1). What is your vision? What do you see? What is it that you really, really need out of life? Does it have purpose?

2). What is persistence? How badly do you want it? What is the purpose? Can you deal with face all the challenges?

3). Do you have the tools of discipline, along with the needed persistence to make your vision a reality?

4). Is your cognitive focus a mental clarity? Are you enhancing your memory supported by physical energy?

5). What is your positive outlook? Do you see yourself as a soaring eagle? Is your positive vision self-less?

6). Have you identified your obstacles? Are you moving your obstacles as stepping stones forward?

7). Are your adversities obstacles? Or are your obstacles adversities? Are you telling the mountain to move? Or are you trying to move the mountain? Is your spiritual guidance being strengthened? Are you meditating as you move forward with your vision?

8). Has your positive attitude become stronger through spiritual guidance, enhanced with continued meditation?

9). Are you defining success as a destination or as a journey? Do you have healthy balance of lifestyle in your journey toward success? Are you maintaining positive focus in your footsteps to success? Success is never final success is maintaining a continued positive focus of "Security Assessment," through lifestyle management.

10). Do you have the courage to continue the success journey? Are you stepping-up to the responsibilities of success?

11). Have you opened-up to the boundless opportunities that life has to offer you? Are you sharing the opportunities? Are you researching the bounty of additional opened opportunities by working smarter rather than harder?

12). Are your goal(s) defined by your "vision?" Have you given your goal(s) have objectives toward a stated mission? Is the defined objective reasonable and realist? Or is it a dream deferred? Is the stated mission objectionable? How does the goal reach the stated mission objective?

Focus on these 12 Steps to select your "Life Style Management" Theme!!! Keep Focused!!! Keep Focused!! Think Positive Factors!!

Body Language Becoming a Better

This session consist of mental exercise combination of "Body Language," "Becoming a Better You Workshop," and "Commentary." When becoming a "New You," mental focus exercises will gear Mind/Body /Spirit = Meditation to a Healthy Balance Life Style.

- Success - Never, Never, Never Quit!

- Determination - Some Succeed Because They Are Destined To, But Most Succeed Because They Are Determined To!

- Achievement - The Starting Point For All Achievement Is Desire. Keep This Constantly In Mind!

- Challenge - Push yourself Again And Again. Don't Give An Inch Until The Final Buzzer Sounds!

- S D A C - Success, Determination, Achievement, and Challenge.............

```
***********************************************************
***********************************************************
***********************************************************
*
```
Meditation means mental focus within your body and your spirit......A mental picture of success, a mental picture of determination, a mental picture of achievement and a mental picture of challenge within your total being within your dream!

S D A C, total mental body language becoming a new you, a better you............
```
***********************************************************
***********************************************************
***********************************************************
*
```

"Words to Meditate Upon"

"If we all did things we are capable of doing, we would

literally astound ourselves................"

"The successful man will profit from his mistakes and try again........."

"Whether you think you can or you think you can't, you're right........."

"The quality of a person's life is in the direct proportion to their commitment to excellence......"

"Persistence and determination alone are omnipotent."

"A noble person attracts noble people, and knows how to hold onto them..........."

"Strength does not come from physical capacity. It comes from indomitable will..."

"No one can make you feel inferior without your consent......"

"Chance favors the prepared mind.................."

"Always do more than is required of you..........."

"You hit home runs not by chance but, by preparation...this is a chance for you to
do your best and to be you're.............."

"The path to success is to take massive, determined action......................"

"When you come to the end of your rope, tie a knot and hang on.................."

"Every man is the architect of his own fortune...."

"Never despair, keeping pushing on..............."

"Do the very best you know how, the very best you can, and keep on doing it to the end............"

"You'll never be a loser until you quit trying...."

"You will become as small as your controlling desire, as great as your dominant aspiration......"

"The first and most important step toward success is the feeling that we can succeed.............."

"Little minds are tamed and subdued by misfortune, but great minds rise above them.............."

"Hit the ball over the fence and you can take your time going around the bases..."

"The starting point for all achievement is desire. Keep this constantly in mind."

"The highest reward for a person's toil is not what he gets for it, but what he becomes by it."

"Hard work has made it easy. That is the secret. That is the will of a winner...."

"Need and struggle are what excite and inspire us."

"A person's dreams are an index to their greatness."

"Do your best brilliantly and the cream will rise to the top...................."

"Try out your ideas by visualizing them in action."

"You win only if you aren't afraid to lose......."

"What a person does tells us who they are........."

"Never give up then, for that is just the place and

time that the tide will turn."

"Always try to turn every disaster into an opportunity. ..."

"It is hard to fail, but it is worse never to have tried to succeed............."

"The thing that contributes to anyone reaching a goal is simply wanting that goal badly enough....."

"Never walk away from failure. On the contrary, study it carefully for its hidden assets.........."

"Try not to become an individual of success but rather a person of value........."

"Nothing can add more power to your life than concentrating all of your energies on a limited set of targeted objectives............."

"Progress always involves risk; you can't stay; second base and keep your foot on first..........."

"If you want a thing done well, do it yourself...."

"You can preach a better sermon with your life than with your lips................"

"Like what you do. If you don't like it, do something else......................."

"What happens is not as important as how you react to what happens..............."

"Success is a state of mind. If you want success, start thinking of yourself as a success..........."

"Goals are dreams we convert to plan and take action to fulfill................."

"If you don't know where you are going, you will probably wind up somewhere else."

"There are no gains without pains...............Excellence

Networking**********

Networking is not easy to start for anyone, whether you are naturally gregarious or terrifically shy. It pulls us out of our comfort zone because it makes us vulnerable to others. Yet, acceptance and or rejection are as much a part of networking as job interviewing. Certainly, it's likely that some people you are reaching out to may not be able to or want to help. Other people may surprise you will how much they do help.

Believe it or not, getting rejections can be a good sign. It can mean you are doing your job! Let me tell you about a salesman who loved rejection. He was known to be quite pleased after he left a business that turned down his product. Why, you ask. Was he crazy? No, not at all. What this very rational man knew was that winning a sale was the realization of a statistical probability. He knew that it took a number of rejections before a sale came through. By viewing life this way, as it actually is, he was able to keep an upbeat attitude that contributed to his successful sales record.

We all need that perspective. As a beginning networker, you have lots of people to call. Not everyone is going to help. Statistically, though, it's quite probable that some people will be delighted to help. Along the same lines, of those who spend time with you, not everyone is going to have worthwhile advice. Yet, statistically, there are going to be some great nuggets of advice coming your way.

The next time you are at a networking event, here are some steps to take to focus in on the right people, people you
should be glad to owe indebtedness.

Don't try to talk with everyone. Your goal is not to return home with everyone's business cards. So, you will need to
spend some time talking with people, assessing their capacity and willingness to become part of your network.

Rehearse your main points in advance. If you're shy, you are also likely to be detail oriented. Use this to your advantage by customizing your "pitch" to your networking contacts as they will all have different ways they may be able to help.

Remember, it's okay to be uncomfortable reaching out to strangers. Most people are flattered if someone approaches them in the right way. One day a very enterprising person called me and even though I was very busy, she convinced me to go to lunch with her. For lunch, this woman arrived dressed for a job interview, making me feel that she valued the time I took with her. About half way through the meeting, I found her to be smart and resourceful. Had I known of a job, I certainly would have passed along the news to her. A few months later, her photo in the newspaper's business section accompanied an announcement of her great new job. Who knows how many rejections she encountered or how much time she spent being uncomfortable. In the end, it all paid off.

Be patient. Be prepared to spend a lot of time developing your network. It's not realistic to believe that you're going to receive enough valuable job leads from a single or even a few networking sessions. Also, don't expect new acquaintances to give you recommendations to their trusted peers if they have just met you. It takes time to build trust.

Set goals that work for you. Remember that it's better to reach out to a handful of people each day than nobody at all. This isn't an all-or-nothing competition. Someone else may be glad-handing dozens of people a day, but it's far better to focus on the quality of your connections than the quantity.

Value what you have. Most shy people are effective listeners. Listening is a key aspect to successful networking. Everyone appreciates the person who remembers their details. If you are a good listener, know that you possess a valuable attribute.

If you are shy, you may need to work on your body language. This means learning how to use good posture to your advantage, how to maintain a comfortable, natural level of eye contact and learning how to smile at the right time. Work with a friend to get feedback on your body language and consult one of the many books on this subject.

Network every day, everywhere follow the demand for your talent by continuous networking, making it second nature. Make your own connections and be your own agent.

There are networking opportunities every day. It's done at parties, dinners, events, small gatherings, birthdays, volunteer activities, and ceremonies. It happens at the gym, the grocery store, and the garage. Talk to anyone and everyone including those new to an industry and old pros, those in school and those overseas. They all matter.

Try this mental game at a networking function. First, bring a stack of business cards at least a quarter inch thick. See if you can find three people who refuse to take one. Chances are, you'll run out of business cards before you find even one person who says no.

Keep an active and pleasant communication open with past employers, being careful not to burn bridges when you leave a company. If you leave the workforce for a few years to raise children, network with other stay-at-home parents and attend your partner's company events at the holidays.

10 Steps to Networking Goals:

1) Choose goals that are worthwhile.

You would think it would go without saying but lots of people set meaningless goals - and then wonder why they don't feel any sense of achievement. Remember that the purpose of goal setting is to move us forward and spur positive change. If a goal doesn't have this motivating, transformational quality, do not bother with it. You'll just be disappointed.

2) Choose goals that are achievable stretches.

The fact that goals have to be achievable is standard goal setting advice. Pretty well everyone knows that there's no point in setting a goal that you will never be able to accomplish. All you'll do is get frustrated and abandon it. Less well known is the fact that goals need to stretch you in some fashion. If a goal isn't engaging, you'll get bored and abandon it. (See 3 Rules for Setting Business Goals for more on this.)

3) Make your goals specific.

The big problem with the sample goals I've used to open this article is that they're vague. To decide that you're going to lose twenty pounds, for instance, is nice, but provides you with no guidance for doing that. Think how much easier it would be to accomplish this goal if you knew exactly what you were going to do to lose the weight. So when you're goal setting, use a goal setting formula that gives your goal a built-in action plan. You'll start accomplishing more than you thought possible.

4) Commit to your goals.

You need to dedicate yourself to accomplish the goal you have chosen. That's why writing your goals down is a common goal setting tip; it's the first step to committing to achieving your goals. But you also have to realize that accomplishing a goal is not an overnight process and that you are going to have to work regularly at transforming your goal into an accomplishment. And you have to set aside the time you will need to work on your goal.

5) Make your goal public.

Making your goal public is a goal setting technique that is really effective for many people. Think of organizations such as TOPS (Take Off Pounds Sensibly) and their weekly weigh ins. Knowing that others are going to be monitoring your results ensures commitment to the goal and is extremely motivating. You don't have to join an organization or broadcast your goal on a Facebook page to make your goal public; having a goal buddy, a single person interested in your efforts, can be just as effective. So far we've looked at how you can set the right goals, and the importance of making your goals specific and committing to working on them. Here are five more goal setting tips to help you accomplish what you want to accomplish.

6) Prioritize your goals.

Goals don't have to be huge projects that take months or even years to attain, but because they require commitment and need to be worked on regularly, every single goal that you set will be demanding. So don't sabotage yourself by taking on a bunch of goals at a time. Assuming that you are following all the other goal setting tips presented here and setting goals that are worthwhile, I would recommend working on no more than three at a time, and even then you should choose one goal as your top priority.

7) Make your goals real to you.

Goal setting is basically a way to approach the process of accomplishment. It's a very successful way, if done right, but like all such processes, it's a bit abstract. Using techniques such as visualization to focus on what actually accomplishing your goal will be like and what it will do for you can be very powerful - and a great help in staying motivated. Choosing and posting pictures that represent successfully accomplishing your goal is another way of doing this.

8) Set deadlines to accomplish your goals.

A goal without a deadline is a goal that you have not fully committed to and a goal you will not achieve. For one thing, if working on achieving a goal is something you can do whenever, you won't. For another, having a deadline will shape your plan of action. To return to the weight loss example, it makes a great difference whether your goal is to lose twenty pounds in four months or in ten. You will have to do a lot more exercising and cutting down of your food portions if you want to lose the weight more quickly.

9) Evaluate your goals.

Remember that goal setting is a process - and evaluation is an important part of that process. Do not just settle for a 'good' or 'bad' assessment; think about what you did, how you did it and what you got out of it. Whether you successfully accomplished your goal or not, there's always something to be learned; what works or doesn't work for you, whether achieving your goal lived up to your expectations, why you failed. Extracting these lessons will increase your accomplishments even more as you apply them to your future goal setting experience.

10) Reward yourself for accomplishment.

Internal satisfaction is a great thing, but external rewards can be immensely satisfying, too. When you accomplish a goal, you've devoted time and effort to your success, so take the time to celebrate your success, too. One caveat; don't undermine your efforts by choosing an inappropriate reward. Eating a huge slab of cheesecake is not an appropriate reward for losing twenty pounds; for example, a new outfit would be a more suitable choice.

Set the Stage for Your Goal Setting Success...

So don't defeat your goal setting efforts before you even start to work on accomplishing your desired goals. Set yourself up for success rather than failure by applying these ten goal setting tips and start achieving what you want to achieve.

Professionals in

the City Organization:

Professionals in the City is a socializing and networking organization that offers professionals in major cities an opportunity to unwind, have fun, and meet people who share their interests.

This established company sets a new standard. They strive to offer original and amazing events every single week. A typical event ranges from as few as 20 to over 2,000 attendees. They hope you will join them and our over 100,000 current members.

They organize over 1,000 great events each year to bring the local professional community together and familiarize residents with all the excitement their city has to offer. From happy hours, to theme parties at the best clubs and restaurants, to embassy galas, to sporting events, to outdoor activities and tours, to educational seminars, to trips to foreign countries, there is something for everyone. Whether you are interested in exchanging business tips, learning or trying something new, exploring the city, or finding friends or romance, Professionals in the City hosts a variety of events for individuals like you.

As a member, you will be able to participate in a variety of entertaining activities with your fellow professionals without having to go through the trouble of planning them yourself. Most of the members are between the ages of 25 and 39; if you fall outside this age range, you are more than welcome to attend the events. They also hold events specifically for people ages 21 to 29 and for people ages 35 and up.

Although they host some singles events, they are not a singles organization. Many individuals come to the events alone, with friends, with spouses or significant others, or with people they have met at prior Professionals in the City events.

Becoming a member is fast and easy. All you have to do is sign up once to receive their weekly emails. From then on, membership is free and you will be kept up-to-date on all the wonderful opportunities being planned in your area.

They also host private events for corporations and individuals. If you are interested in hosting a private event, please email them at dc@prosinthecity.com.

==Frequently Asked Questions about Professions in the City:==

What makes Professionals in the City events unique?

First, they plan events that they know people would enjoy attending with their friends, colleagues, and significant others if they had the means to organize them on their own. Second, by monitoring what's hot in and around the city, they hold their events at only the best venues and locations. Third, our experienced and professional staff members are always present as hosts, ensuring the success of each gathering. They are sure to surpass your expectations by providing high quality events that enable you to meet a variety of new people and explore the city and surrounding areas.

How do I become a member?

Just sign up for free on the top of our homepage or click here to sign up for our email list. Once you sign up, you automatically become a member.

How much does it cost to join?

Nothin. Membership is free once you sign up for our weekly emails.

What are the advantages of becoming a member?

Besides keeping you up-to-date through their weekly emails with exciting events to participate in with old friends, new friends and significant others, they save your contact information to speed up future ordering and make it easy for you to stay involved.

I signed up to join your list but never received an email. What now?

Contact them via email: dc@prosinthecity.com to let us know. Also, please add this email address to your Address Book to prevent their messages from being blocked by Spam filters.

What are the members like?

Professionals in the City are a diverse group of individuals from an array of backgrounds, experiences, and professions. All of them share the desire to have a good time and meet other professionals in the area. Just go to events that you enjoy, and you will meet people that share your interests.

What is the age range of your members?

They have different groups covering different age ranges. Their core group is comprised of individuals primarily between the ages of 25 and 39, but they also hold separate events for people ages 21 to 29 and for people ages 35 and up. Here is the breakdown of our three age groups:

Young Professionals in the City (Ages 21 - 29)

Professionals in the City (Ages 25 - 39)
Seasoned Professionals in the City (Ages 35 Plus)

Do I have to attend events for my age range?

No. The age ranges are simply suggested parameters to help you find the group most suitable for you and the events that you will feel most comfortable attending. You are welcome to attend any event. They also sometimes offer events that overlap two suggested age ranges or that cover only part of a suggested age range.

Do I have to be single?

Many of the members are single, but it is certainly not a requirement. Couples and groups of friends are welcome to attend the events together. Approximately 70 percent of the members are single and 30 percent are in relationships.

Do I have to live or work in the city to join your organization?

Of course not! If you know that you will be traveling and want to have some fun and meet people in a city you are visiting, they encourage you to check the website in advance to find events that interest you.

I don't know anyone in Professionals in the City. Can I attend events alone?

Absolutely! In fact, the majority of the members do so, which is why it is our aim to create a comfortable and enjoyable environment for all you professionals to meet and get to know each other. In fact, if you let them know when you check in that you would like to be introduced around, they will introduce you to other people who have made a similar request.

How do I sign up for an event I want to attend?

Just click on our Order Form button or click here. They accept Visa, MasterCard, American Express, and Discover through our secure server. You will receive a confirmation email shortly after your information is processed. If you do not receive a confirmation, it could be that your ISP is blocking our emails from getting through to you. You can always log on to their website to confirm which events you are signed up for. You can also purchase tickets by calling 202-686-5990 or contacting them at dc@prosinthecity.com to find out where you can send a check made out to Professionals in the City. They do accept cash at the door for some of their events, but if you decide not to purchase tickets in advance they cannot guarantee that space will be available. Also, the price is frequently higher at the door than it is for advance purchases.

If I reach a voicemail message when I call the PNC line, when can I expect my call to be returned?

If you reach their voicemail, please leave a message. We check our voicemail regularly, and someone will promptly return your call. You can usually expect a call back from us within two hours of leaving your message.

What happens if I am late or miss an event that I already paid for?

They apologize, but we cannot give you a refund or credit if you sign up for an event and are unable to attend at the last minute. This is true even if you are ill, hit traffic, have a personal emergency, or otherwise are unable to attend the event. The reason for this is that they are normally required to pay for your presence in advance.

Since they do not offer refunds or credits, please

allocate enough time so that you do not miss out on the fun. If you cannot attend an event, you are welcome to transfer your ticket for that event to somebody else. Just let them know in advance the name of the person you want to transfer your ticket to. The only time they cannot permit ticket transfers is when they are prohibited from doing so, which happens sometimes with airline tickets, certain embassies that require advance security checks on all names, and similar activities.

Do you mail tickets?

No. they put your name on a list that their representatives use to check you in at the door. They also email you a confirmation when you place your order, and they request that you bring a printout of your confirmation to the event. They suggest adding them to your Address Book so that confirmations do not end up in your Junk Folder as a result of SPAM filters.

What do I do if I have a great idea for an event?

They would love to hear your ideas. If your recommended event is something that they think most of the members would enjoy, they will try our best to make it happen. Feel free to email your thoughts to us at dc@prosinthecity.com.

How do I know if an event is cancelled due to rain or other poor weather?

If you are in doubt about the weather for an event, please check our website or check our voicemail at 202-686-5990,in the Washington DC headquarters office. If this event is postponed due to adverse weather, the website and outgoing recording will both, state that this event has been postponed due to adverse weather. If the website and our outgoing recording do not both explicitly state that the event has been postponed due to adverse weather, it means that this event is still going on a scheduled.............

Who do I contact with other questions?

Email at dc@prosinthecity.com. Headquarters in Washington DC

Events in Other Cities

Atlanta
Baltimore
Boston
Cleveland
Chicago
Dallas
Denver
Los Angeles
Miami
New York
Philadelphia
Portland
San Francisco
Seattle

Swap Shopping

Swap Shopping is an economical way to get what you need and maintain what you need on a budget without costing you money a lot of money. Invest your time in "Swap Shopping," because time is money..........................

==Online Swap Shopping - About Favorpals.com==

Favorpals is response to the untapped potential for mutual benefit that we see in the connections billions of people are making on the World Wide Web every day. The company is dedicated to the belief that human beings can better serve each other through a spirit of collective cooperation......

Begin by imagining that money ceases to be the currency of choice. Imagine you can have almost anything you want without having to reach into your pocket for your wallet. What if the billions of online users can make this happen?

==Welcome to the world of Favorpals a money-free system of exchange:==

Favorpals provides the space where services can be freely exchanged for other services and/or goods" all without engaging in a traditional monetary transaction.

Craftsmen, artists, laborers, professionals" in fact anyone with skills or goods to trade can swap for the services or items they need with anyone in the Favorpals community. And because of the wide reach of the Web, they can make an exchange with someone around the corner or even a continent way......................

Favorpals.com "swaps" as an especially meaningful event when the exchange crosses the divide between people from different walks of life, where both parties benefit equally regardless of class or status....................................

When using the website, please remember that the intention is not just to get a good deal but also to give.................

FREQUENTLY ASKED QUESTIONS about Favorpal.com

What is Favorpals?

Favorpals is a services-exchange community. They believe that everyone in the world is good at something. They also believe that everyone, once in a while, needs help with a thing or two. Imagine somewhere perhaps far from physical reach but within range you can find another person willing to trade services with you in an even exchange. Imagine that what you can do is as valuable as what they can offer to do in return. This is the world of Favorpals.

What do we exchange?

Simply, they facilitate the direct exchange of services to services. As a community holding to the ideal of a pure favor exchange, they guard against the biggest sin of all (mis)use of the m-word; absolutely nothing may be exchanged for money. No member may even mention monetary value in connection with the exchange of services.

I've signed up and have not yet received my confirmation email. Where is my confirmation email?

Your confirmation email may have been delivered your spam folder. Please go to your spam folder, and mark the email as not a spam. To avoid emails from favorpals ending up in the spam folder you can also add admin@favorpals.com to your address book.

How does it work?

It's simple! Imagine that money does not exist, or if that's too difficult then imagine that you can circumvent the concept of monetary value. Imagine all skill sets are created equal. I can fix your leaky faucet if you mow my lawn; or, better yet, I can fix your faucet if you do my root canal surgery you get the idea. Favorpals.com allows you to create a profile, search for or list the favor you want, and describe the favor you can provide in return.

How do you value different services?

All services can be equated to a single unit of service. All UOS are equal. A single dental filling is equivalent to a single tax filing, which is equivalent to a single gardening session, and the list goes on. Naturally it will be up to the parties exchanging the favors to determine an agreed-upon UOS. However, the best way to classify a UOS is to think of it as the amount of work needed to complete a service. For example, if you are offering house cleaning, a UOS would be to clean the whole house once. Cleaning three quarter of the house is not a complete UOS, cleaning the house once a week is a recurring UOS, and so on.

How do I request a favor?

Easy, simple, and free:

- Register
- Write your favor request
- Write what you can offer in exchange

That's it............................

Take a minute to register, select your city, and find a suitable category. If one does not exist, select "other" and enter your favor. Try to be as descriptive as possible so other members can respond accurately. It also helps to list your neighborhood if your request requires a physical meeting...........

Don't forget to list what favor you're offering; there will be no freebies, you're paying in services.

Wait for a response. You will receive an e-mail from them any time a member of the Favorpals.com community has responded.

If I have to perform my service first, how do I guarantee that the other member will reciprocate?

While swapping is an excellent way to obtain services without monetary cost, it relies upon the honesty of the participants. A dishonest participant might arrange a swap and then never complete their end of the transaction, thus getting something for nothing. This practice is called swap-shopping................................

After you exchange a favor with another Favorpals.com member, please take a moment to rate your experience using the Favorpals.com rating system. This helps the community regulate itself and weeds out those who might take advantage of our system. The rating systems will not only help the community identify and ban swap-shoppers, but it would also help us recognize the most reliable members....

Also, when considering a favor exchanges use your best judgment before making the agreement much as you would for anything else in life really.

Who can join Favorpals?

Anyone who understands and shares our ideal; Favorpals benefits all people and organizations that recognize the mutual benefit in exchanging services rather than currency. It also enables those who lack "hard currency" to obtain services they could not otherwise afford. Please join our community and help nurture this simple yet ingenuous economic system.

Are there any tax implications for services that are exchanged?

In the United States it is generally expected that income taxes are owed on an exchange of services. According to the IRS: "The fair market value of goods and services exchanged must be included in the income of both parties;" The recipient of the service is expected to report its value on Form 1099-B and Schedule C. Favorpals take no responsibilities for income taxes accrued on any exchange made on its site.

May I have my own private network to exchange favors?

Are there any restrictions on favors that may be exchanged?

They reserve the right to remove favors that the Favorpals community deems inappropriate.

How Do You Win & Influence People???/Advance Development

-

Part One. Fundamental Techniques in Handling People

1. If You Want to Gather Honey, Don't Kick Over the

Beehive.

Here is an important principle in relationships: do not criticize, condemn or complain. People rarely blame themselves for anything, so if you criticize them not only are they unlikely to change, but also they may resent toward you.

2. The Big Secret of Dealing with People:

People will go long way - sometimes even become insane - just to get the appreciation they need. So be a person who gives honest and sincere appreciation to others. That's the big secret of dealing with people. If you do that, you can't keep people from liking you.

Part Two. Six Ways to Make People Like You

1. Do This And You'll be Welcome Anywhere:

You can make more friends in two months by becoming interested in other people than you can in two years by trying to get other people interested in you.

Are you interested in others? Do you want to know about them, admire their work, and eager to help them? If you do, they will also be interested in you.

2. A Simple Way to Make a Good First Impression:

The way to make a good first impression is so simple that we sometimes forget it: smile. When you smile, people will feel that you are glad to meet them. They will feel accepted and get a good first impression about you.

3. If You Don't Do This, You Are Headed for Trouble:

People put tremendous importance on their names. Therefore it will be much easier for you to win their hearts if you approach them by using their names. Unfortunately, we often forget names.

I am as guilty as anybody else here. Sometimes I am introduced to someone only to forget his or her name right after the conversation. Another embarrassing situation is when I meet someone who calls me by name but whose name I forget.

4. An Easy Way to Become a Good Conversationalist:

It may seem counterintuitive, but being a good conversationalist is about by how good you talk. It's about how good you listen. Encourage others to talk about themselves and be a good listener. People will feel appreciated and they will
regard you as a nice people to talk with.

6. How to Make People Like You Instantly:

To make people like you, make them feel important and do it sincerely. The desire to feel important is perhaps the
deepest need someone has, so if you give it you will win their heart.

I wrote some practical tips on Becoming a Well Liked Person.

Part Three. How to Win People to Your Way of Thinking

1. You Can't Win an Argument:

You can only lose if you argue because - no matter what the outcome of the argumentation is - you won't win their heart.
So the way to get the best of an argument is to avoid it.

This is something that is rather difficult for me. If I have an idea I am confident about, I am usually willing to
argue to prove my point. This chapter shows me how wrong it is.

2. If You Must Find Fault, begin with yourself...........

3. A Sure Way of Making Enemies - And How to Avoid It:

A sure way of making enemies is by saying that they are wrong. People do not like that, regardless of whether they are actually wrong or not. Such statements hurt their self-esteem. So learn to respect other people's opinion, even when you disagree.

4. The Secret of Socrates:

If you want to win other people to your way of thinking, it's important to make them agree with you from the beginning. The way to do that is by asking questions that they will inevitably answer with one another. Every time they say anything they will become more receptive toward you. At the end, there is a good chance that they will accept the idea they previously rejected. This is a technique used by Socrates to convince his opponents.

5. A Formula that Will Work Wonders for You:

There must be a reason why people say or act the way they do. Find that reason and talk from their point of view. If you understand them, they will in turn understand you.

Part Four - Be a Leader Without Giving Offense or Arousing Resentment.

As a leader, we sometimes need to correct the people we

lead. But how can we do that without offending them? The answer is by praising and giving honest appreciation first. When we do that, they will become much more receptive to the correction we give.

6. How to Spur People On to Success:

The best way to develop good traits in others is not by punishing them for incorrect actions but by rewarding them for correct actions. Praise every improvement they make, even the slightest one, and they will go to the right direction.

7. Give a Dog a Good Name:

A good way to get others do things the way you want it is by giving them a fine reputation to live up to. For instance, if you want someone to be diligent then treat her as a diligent person and say so to her. Most likely she won't disappoint you.

In Conclusion:

How to Win Friends and Influence People contains excellent principles for human relations. The principles are universal and cover practically every important aspect of relationships. The stories in each chapter make it easy to grasp those principles.

The problem, of course, is in putting the principles into practice. Knowing the principles is one thing, but applying them is another thing. Since most of us have the tendency to be selfish, we need conscious and serious effort to apply these principles in LifeStyle Management - Profession and Personal Development with SA-Security Assessment.

Turning the art of assertiveness into a simple science will win friends and influence people:

Maybe you think, like many people, that being assertive is just a fancy word for being cutthroat … getting what you want at all costs … and taking down anyone who stands in your way.

Actually, that's aggressive behavior, and for the most part, it's not very effective at all. Not in the long run, at least. And its polar opposite, passivity, is equally ineffective.

True assertiveness is the art of holding firm in your beliefs, desires, and needs, without diminishing the beliefs, desires, or needs of another. Sound tough?

It won't be, once you learn the five essential skills that will unlock this power within you. You will literally have people lining up at your door to help you succeed.

In fact, this program turns what can be an elusive art into a simple science by providing you with a structure and system for understanding exactly how to unleash appropriate assertiveness in any situation.

Easy-to-learn skills that will put you at the top of your game You see, business leaders who practice true assertiveness have people cheering for them when they make it to the top because they get there by playing fair, valuing not only their own contributions, but those of everyone who helped them succeed along the way.

Today, Oprah Winfrey is the embodiment of assertiveness. Her famous ability to empathize with her guests and viewers inspires the trust and admiration of millions.

But she's also no stranger to controversy or cut-throat business tactics, as shown when she was taken to court by the beef industry or the many shows that have sparked anger in others — that she has had to stand up and answer for.

Through it all, her command of the five essential skills of assertiveness has helped her handle every challenge, take advantage of every opportunity, and gracefully accept every honor that has come her way in a manner that most of us would agree makes her one of today's most powerful business leaders.

You'll be amazed at how simple it will be for you to identify these same assertive behaviors and responses — and start practicing them immediately — when you listen to this program just once.

Then, after you repeat it a second, and maybe even a third time, you will take your grasp of the skills to a level of mastery. Here are just a few things you'll be able to do after you learn, The Essential People Skills: How to Assert Yourself, Listen to Others, and Resolve Conflict:

- Handle high-stress, high-stakes interactions with ease and confidence

- Learn how to stand your ground without alienating the other person

- Create an atmosphere of equality and mutual respect that inspires everyone to do his or her best work

- Understand how different personality types operate, and how you can develop solid relationships with every one of them......

- Develop a mutual liking and trust with your colleagues that lays the groundwork for boundless success in all your business endeavors.......

- Deliver negative feedback so artfully that the other person will thank you for your support.......

- Apply communications will virtually assure you will get great results usually better than what you'd hoped for......

- Set yourself free from the pressure of having to know all the answers and learn instead how asking the right questions can lead to creative solutions to the toughest problems.......

- Discover the key to motivating yourself and others to take on new challenges and break new ground, not just put in a day's work for a day's pay.......

- Experience the power of leading by example and harness the positive energy of ambition in your entire team. Be an example of the change you want from others, and watch them rise to the occasion to meet you.......

- Find a positive solution to any conflict that ensures the real needs of all parties are met and the conflict won't reignite the minute that you move on to other things.......

######Fundamental Techniques in Handling People######

- Don't criticize, condemn or complain.
- Give honest and sincere appreciation.
- Arouse in the other person an eager want.

#####Six Ways to Make People Like You#####

Become genuinely interested in other people.

Smile.

Remember that a man's Name is to him the sweetest and most important sound in any language.

Be a good listener. Encourage others to talk about themselves.

Talk in the terms of the other man's interest.

Make the other person feel important and do it sincerely.

　　*****Twelve Ways to Win People to Your Way of Thinking*****

Avoid arguments.

Show respect for the other person's opinions. Never tell someone they are wrong.

If you're wrong, admit it quickly and emphatically.

Begin in a friendly way.

Start with questions the other person will answer yes to.

Let the other person do the talking.

Let the other person feel the idea is his/hers.

Try honestly to see things from the other person's point of view.

Sympathize with the other person.

Appeal to noble motives.

Dramatize your ideas.

Throw down a challenge.

Be a Leader

- How to Change and Influence People Without Giving Offense or Arousing Resentment

- Begin with praise and honest appreciation.

- Call attention to other people's mistakes indirectly.

- Talk about your own mistakes first.

- Ask questions instead of giving direct orders.

- Let the other person save face.

- Praise every improvement!!!

Advanced Development Advanced Self- Development**

Develop a fine reputation to live up

to................

Encouragement!!!!Encouragement!!!!!!!Encouragement!!!!

Make the other person happy about doing what you suggest.

Seven Rules For Making your Life Happier:

Love and Let Live................................

Communication.....Communication......Communication....
....
Look Up the Time-Tables to ......Vacation .....Vacation ....Vacation.....

Look for a quick Way to Make Everybody Happy..............

What Means so Much to a Woman????????????????

If You Want to be Happy, Don't Neglect Yourself and Love Ones........

Don't be a "Marriage Illiterate".................
"Read" a good book on the sexual side of marriage and communication. . . . .

The experience of life is always in your hands. Every moment offers you the free will to choose how you will interpret, react and affect the world around you. This is the essence of the power of the universe that is inside you. May you come to understand this power, claim it, and become a light to others in the world that is looking to experience this understanding for their selves.

Your Truth.....Life is About Living Your Truth.....Truth About Yourself........

Each day of life brings new answers. It is a journey of discovery, personal growth and self-realization that leads
you to understand and know more about who you really are and what you are capable of creating every day.

Life can be filled with many different personal challenges. When resisted or misunderstood, these challenges can end up dominating your life and causing a state of disharmony. This leads to a negative state of mind, energy-draining emotions, and a string of clouded choices that can seem to make the circumstances of your life even worse. Many times this cycle goes on for days that turn into weeks and can end up becoming months. For many in the world, the cycle has been going on for years.

"Right now, if you so choose, you can experience the answers that will end conflict and disharmony and immediately change your life in a very positive way."

Every person looks at the world through a slightly different lens. The result is an accumulation of beliefs started at birth that are your collective truth until challenged and changed. Together, these beliefs shape the thoughts, feelings, and actions that create your moment-by-moment reality. What you believe therefore creates the life you experience, a reality that you determine to be either desired or undesired. As you react to this reality in every moment, you are creating a new reality in the next moment. It is this continuous perception-reaction cycle that is the engine of your experience of life

"You can't change what has happened in your past or how you reacted to any of it. However, you can change the way you react to what is happening NOW, thereby creating the conditions for a new experience in your present and future moments. This is how life changes."

The desire to create or change an aspect of your life requires that you face the truth about what you have previously believed. This is the root of the actions and reactions that have led you to your current experience. The most important question to focus on, as it relates to changing your current experience of life is:

Is my current truth about this issue serving me in creating the reality I desire to experience?

For example:

Is my current truth about my abilities at my job creating the position in the company or the vocation that I desire to have?

Is my current truth about the way I feel about myself creating the love relationship that I long for?

Is my current truth about the way I handle money creating the financial security I envision for my life?

Is my current truth about the way I nurture, discipline, and engage with my children creating the daily relationship with them that I desire?

Is my current truth about the way I treat my body resulting in the physical appearance and well-being that I would like to have?

Is my current truth about my spouse creating the intimacy, connection, trust, and support I would like to experience on a daily basis?

Is my current truth about what I was taught from well meaning parents, teachers, and religious leaders serving me in experiencing daily peace in my life?

Is my current truth about what I believe is possible for me to do with my life creating the daily fulfillment I would like to experience?

Is my current truth about who I am and giving me the life I desire to live?

These examples demonstrate how critical it is to evaluate whether what you believe to be true is serving your ultimate intended desire because it is the key that shapes your experience of life. What should be of great hope and comfort is that YOU are always the in control of the beliefs and truths that end up creating the exact circumstances of your life!

The question is: Are you ready to evaluate, question, and open up to learn something new about you and your life? If you are, then the next step to change comes down to your willingness to accept your answers. What are your life's questions???

Your Answers...Will Appear When You Are True To Yourself.... . . .

If you desire to change your life you will not only have to ask the questions that challenge some of your long held beliefs about you or your world, but you will also have to allow in the answers that may change them. These beliefs have either come from your own personal experiences or from the instruction of others. Mainly well-meaning people, such as your parents, religious leaders, teachers, friends, and relatives have offered information to you in the best way they know how.

Everybody passes on what they believe to be the truth about life to others. Many of the beliefs that they passed to you may, in fact, have been necessary at the time for them and the way they were living their lives, but the may have little or no relevance or benefit to your life now. What is right for one person may be completely wrong for another.

"The truth and answers in life are relative to each individual and what they are trying to accomplish in the world."

Every day many people ask questions, but yet only a small percentage of them are ready to embrace the answers that will give them the clarity to make new choices. It is from these new choices that a new and desired reality gets created.

Change is often feared and resisted. Even if the current circumstance is filled with an immense amount of pain, you may continue to relive it day after day simply because it is the only life you know. This could be recurring relationship troubles, lack of physical care, job problems, body ailments, addictions, money issues, family tensions, or just an overall and persistent depressed, fearful or negative outlook. Until you are truly ready to live your life differently you won't allow the necessary answers in, and you won't take the actions that produce change.

=="Freedom lies in the awareness that right NOW there are millions of different possibilities for you and your life."==

The answers that reveal these possibilities are in front of you every single day. They show up in the situations you encounter, the people you interact with, the movies, books, and music you experience, and your moment-by-moment feelings and emotions...And still, even with the answers all around you, you have to be ready to accept them. Are you ready now?

"Acceptance is the doorway to transformation."

When you finally allow the answers into your consciousness the shift often come with a great sense of relief and well-being. When understanding occurs, it provides you with the clarity to see the pathway of actions to achieving what it is that you ultimately desire. Change starts with a change in the way you believe, feel, and act. It is always up to you, and this is what defines the essence of your free will. "It is the inner path of personal understanding that leads you to a happy, peaceful and fulfilling Reality".

The Power.........The Creative Power Of The Universe Is Within You........

As you open to new answers and new information, your perspective begins to change regarding the way you look at and experience your world. What you believe to be the truth also changes. As a result you see and believe in new possibilities and new choices that you never even considered prior to this expanded state of awareness. Since you can only take action on what you believe is possible, this is a critical step towards real change. Taking action on these new choices is how the conditions change to produce a new reality for you to experience.

As a new more positive energy of understanding and self-identity gets put out into your world, a new more positive energy begins to come back into your life. You are always setting the conditions for your experience of life by the energy of your thoughts and actions. The sooner you can clearly identify the thoughts, truths, and beliefs you use to operate your life that aren't helping you experience what you desire, the sooner you'll be able to contemplate and take action on the new thoughts and beliefs that will create what you desire.

Many of us attempt to start positive change by changing what we experience on the outside. We sometimes rush to quick fix actions, such as changing jobs, changing significant others, changing our material possessions, changing our physical appearance, or using drugs to artificially change our state of mind. This type of a fix rarely lasts.

"A key missed point is that a change in action without a change in understanding and self-awareness will not change
the experience but simply produce the same feelings and experience in a new situation."

What more and more people are finding out through this game of accumulation and change is that this is not what brings one lasting peace. This frustrating cycle eventually leads to the only path left to real change, the inner path. Your true power comes from the understanding that what you believe about yourself and the world is what is behind the creation of your experience of life.

True and lasting change only occurs through a new acceptance and understanding of YOU.............Your reality at any given moment is always a reflection of who you believe that you are. Your life will remain this way until you decide to challenge and change the long held beliefs that have been driving your daily thoughts, choices and actions. Free will affords you this opportunity in every moment.

Your true power lies in your ability to:

- Earnestly ask questions
- Open to a new understanding of what is true and possible for you
- Make new choices and take new actions

No matter what undesired events you are experiencing now, take comfort in knowing that everything has a purpose . What ever you are experiencing and whatever state of mind it is producing, is changeable. People, places, and events come into your life in direct relationship to what you need to learn and understand to reach a state of peace. The most unwanted situations present you with bigger answers to your bigger questions. When you are ready, you will move through any situation and, if you allow yourself to see the answer that it has for you, you will become clearer, more balanced, and more able to handle the next moments of your life. You will be a source of strength and inspiration for others you meet who are experiencing the same types of situations but have yet to find peace.

You are on an incredible journey in this lifetime. Every moment you experience holds the potential for your edification and growth. This website is just one piece of an infinite supply of information that you can tap into each and every day. As always, how much information comes to you and how quickly depends on you. Just remember, the truth of any issue is never denied to anyone who honestly seeks it, and you always have the opportunity to see it and to accept it at your own self-determined pace.

==**"You always hold the power to change and create your experience of life!"**==

- Advancement In Professional & Personal Development/Character Profile
----

What is Advancement In Professional & Personal Development? - The act or process of promoting one's own qualities and abilities................

What You Get From the Pathway to Professional & Personal Development?

Better self-esteem, confidence and personal power......

Promoting emotional, physical and spiritual health; allowing you to be more focused and productive at work..........

Deals with habits that create self-destructive and limiting behaviors........

Build professional pride through rigorous achievement.....

Develop valuable intangibles, such as trust, honesty, security and purpose.

Dramatically improve communication with family and friends to resolve relationship problems......................

Improve communication in your most important personal relationships (Many marriages have been saved when individuals dealt with their professional and personal needs, making it possible to deal with their relationship needs with others)..........

Emotionally intelligent individuals stand out. The ability to empathize, persevere, control impulses, communicate clearly, make thoughtful decisions, solve problems, and work with others earns friends and success. You will live, with more satisfying relationships; To lead a more productive lifestyle, and spur productivity in your professional development.

Attributes like self-awareness and empathy play a huge role in every aspect of life. "We all know that how we feel about ourselves and others can profoundly affect our ability to concentrate, to remember, to think, and to express ourselves," without emotional intelligence you will have difficulty working cooperatively. The role of ethical principles, character traits, and professional values in ethical decision-making is examined and depicted through an integrated and comprehensive model. It provides an illustration of improved decision making.

Professional Character is an ethical responsibility of professionals is to be true to what they believe and know is right. The character of the professional must be one of high caliber. Within the context of character of an individual must belong within the category of a strongly differentiated ethical role. This category requires that there be elevated moral considerations, or morals that are at a higher level than normal. Professionals make decisions that affect lives more directly. This is the reason that their character must be of high quality in strong role differentiation.

AFFIRMATIONS - Affirmations are positive statements of "Truth!" By affirming Truth, we are lifted out of false thinking into the consciousness of "Spirit!" Each time we mediate or pray faithfully, we are calling forth the divine activity that is always within us........

CHOICES - I listen...I know that I know...If it doesn't feed me, I can choose differently. If it pains me, I can walk away.....If it fills my heart with joy, I can spend
More, time with it.....It is my life....The choices are mine..................

THE KEYS TO SUCCESS - "I am involved in creating my success and happiness! With the awareness of choice, I bring blessings into my life. I am no longer a puppet dangling from a divine string, but rather a player, a divine player, in my life. I call this "divine intention!" I have
the power to change my life............................

NEW DAY - I enter a new day with enthusiasm! This is a new day at the start of something new! I choose to be free of the limiting thoughts of the past and to not allow outworn habits or beliefs to control my life. Perhaps, I'm guided to try something I have not tried before or go somewhere I've never been. If so, I open my mind to divine direction and guidance, and I accept these new experiences as loving gifts. I look for and find the blessings they bring --- blessings of new relationships, hidden talents and the fullness of success...I am excited about this new beginning...my life is brimming with unlimited possibilities for good..............

CREATIVITY - I design my life in cooperation with the Divine....What do I truly love to do? Maybe it's dancing, singing or playing the guitar...Perhaps, it's drawing, painting or woodworking. Whatever the activity, I set the intention to add it to my daily or weekly routine...Creative expression lifts the spirit and energizes our life. As I allow my creativity to shine, I have a renewed zest for life.

My mind and body are recharged and fully engaged as I tune in to the power of Spirit! I let this power radiate through me in new ways........I enjoy rich and abundant living as I open to the continual flow of divine ideas that spring forth from within me.........................

I BELIEVE - There is only One Power and One Presence in believing that I will do good......We are never alone, there is no challenge or opportunity that is beyond trusting in the power of belief, and I am free of fear and apprehension ....No entity, person or situation has the power to negate the goodness within me. Knowing this is true, I am strong and resilient. As I acknowledge and affirm the presence and power in me, in others and in every circumstance, I tap into the all-ness of that is continuously bringing forth blessings. I live life with certainty and enthusiasm! Let the power of belief live in my universe.

GRACE - I am gently supported by grace...It is invisible and mysterious, yet ever present. In times of need I may resist inner guidance and find myself struggling to make progress. Whatever the need, when I turn within to the indwelling presence, I know that through grace, I will receive the answer....Grace gently correct my course and allows me to overcome any troubles. Even in the stormiest of times, I can be lifted above the gusty winds on a gentle current of air that carries me forward....Grace is divine favor offered unconditionally. It is life-giving and ever present. Grace inspires, empowers and propels toward most heartfelt desire. From supported fullness we have all received, grace upon grace...................

DIVINE ORDER - I open my spiritual vision to divine order within and around me...When you think of divine order, you are minded of the exquisite order in nature. From the smallest atom to the tallest mountain, order is evident in nature Creating and supporting life, providing nourishment and shelter, and blessing all people with beauty.....The divine order evident in nature is also
At work in your life, it presents opportunities for growth and renewal, Introduces ideas and inspiration, provides guidance and protection. Divine order blesses us with all we need for a healthy, happy, and productive Life.... ...Right now, opens your spiritual vision to see divine order. Give thanks for the opportunities available to you. Know that the spirit is at work in your life and all life....it is the light of your soul.....

PRAYING FOR OTHERS - Life-affirming thoughts of others are silent prayers reaching out to bless them in positive ways. No matter what others are going through, support them in prayer. Affirmations of Truth are the Foundation of prayers. The power release through affirmations establishes Truth in our consciousness ....Conscious of others enters into the Presence in prayer. In this way, we embrace others, near and far. Hold each one tenderly in our hearts and in our thoughts, affirming their good through the power of prayer.....

PROSPERITY - Claim good...The Universe is boundless! Give thanks for the beauty and Bounty of Earth, for the variety of life it sustains and for our planet's Capacity to replenish and rejuvenate itself....A basic spiritual principle States that good is everywhere present, and everywhere you look, see that This is true. One person smiles at another and the other person smiles back.
A customer exchanges money for goods; the customer proper's, the cashier Prospers, and the shop owner prospers. A child invites another to play his or Her toys, and both children have more fun....As you give to others, it opens the way to greater blessings through the principles of Spirit. The Universe is boundless, and you claim and contribute to your good now......of boundless
Riches of prosperity....................

VITALITY - We are well-nourished, healthy and filled with energy....We are created in the Image of wholeness, strength and vitality---This is the Truth of our being, the
Blueprint of perfection at the core of us all; Consciously focus thoughts, words and actions on this Truth and aligns us with true potential.............Visualizing yourself moving freely and easily, Praise your body and show it respect and appreciation; Living from consciousness of well-being and wholeness, we continually in the flow of divine, life-sustaining energy. We are forever grateful for abundant life, health and guidance in the care of our

Body. Give thanks for our creation to thrive and to flourish..........

NEW DAWN - The light of dawn is in you today and every day! Each morning is a sacred opportunity to begin life anew. Before you rise, spend a moment in appreciation of and reverence for life. The fact that we've awakened tells us that life has yet another opportunity for us.....Walk your chosen path of righteousness, which means right thinking and right understanding. This day, choose to share your joy shine your light brightly as the light and love dawns in you.....Also, see a Dawning of greater spiritual understanding for all people. Though we may be On different paths, we are all expressions of the universe. Because the love in Lives in us, share the love with others unconditionally....But the path of the righteous is like the light of dawn, which shines brighter and brighter until
full day.......

NEW DAWN - The light of dawn is in you today and every day! Each morning is a sacred opportunity to begin life anew. Before you rise, spend a moment in appreciation of and reverence for life. The fact that we've awakened tells us that life has yet another opportunity for us.....Walk your chosen path of righteousness, which means right thinking and right understanding. This day, choose to share your joy shine your light brightly as the light and love dawns in you.....Also, see a Dawning of greater spiritual understanding for all people. Though we may be On different paths, we are all expressions of the universe. Because the love in Lives in us, share the love with others unconditionally....But the path of the righteous is like the light of dawn, which shines brighter and brighter until
full day.......

INNER PEACE - In the silence there is presence within,

you can find peace...Each day can be more peaceful when we spend time in meditation, contemplation and prayer. Closing your eyes, turn within and gently disconnect from any concerns that might be weighing on your mind. Breathe into the peace of the presence within....Completely relax your body and mind.....Affirming divine life, know the wholeness of true nature. Affirming divine substance, know all Good things are right here, right now. Affirming the light of Spirit, guidance is assured. In this conscious awareness, find peace. Abide in peace for long moments of silence, which energizes and prepares us for the rest of the day. Whatever is ahead for the day, you will be calm and serene.

JOY - The spirit of joy sets us free.....Laughter is contagious. When you hear others Laughing freely and wholeheartedly, you are pulled into the fun. Even in tender moments, you find precious release in the joy of laughter and in the joy within. Spirit within is our constant source of joy. At any moment you can tap into the
Joy of simply being alive and experience true happiness in our oneness; Whatever You are doing, the certainty of joyful presence is always within.....Share joy by expressing it in all you do, Joyful experience ae created in your life and in the lives of others because you live from the joy in your heart.......

THIS MOMENT - You are living an abundant life now! Living joyful in the present moment, we make adjustments, changes and choices that enrich life and prepare us for success. We are stress-free as we ease through each day, grateful for   every experience and the blessings it holds....Each moment that we are fully present to the spirit is a moment when we are conscious of divine intelligence and conscious of the ways in which we express our highest potential. We are learning from the Creator and realizing our dreams ....Living in the now, we are not inhibited by time. Let your present experiences flow as if they were taking us on a journey. Every turn offers us another amazing perspective on abundant living....................

SHINE - Let your divine light shine...If shyness, self-critic or any other personality trait is interfering with our enjoyment of life; it may be that certain characteristics no longer serve us. We are free to adopt a new way of being. To accomplish this, we begin by noticing qualities in others that we admire and wish to adopt. We observe another's light and magnetism. We look for someone who models self-acceptance and confidence. We appreciate how they carry themselves with this beautiful presence.....Because these are qualities we admire, they are also qualities found with us...By recognizing our inherent value we, begin to let our light shine bigger and brighter. We express the indwelling Spirit in unique and
Beautiful ways................

HEALING - Health and wholeness are expressing in you now....The healing power of the Spirit is ever present in us. When we are dealing with a health challenge, we may forget this truth. But as we center ourselves on the power of Life in us, we are intensely aware of the healing energy of Spirit....We no longer fixate on what appears to be wrong, but instead see what is true, what is possible. Instead of seeing outer imperfections, we look within and remember our innate perfection.....The wholeness in which we were created is the true nature of our being. From this truth, we can affirm a return to complete healing. We bless our body in its current state, knowing that all is well. We see ourselves through the eyes of Spirit, and smile.....

FORGIVE - When we forgive we are whole...When even one sheep strays from the flock, the shepherd searches to bring it safely back. As a daily practice we search our thoughts to see if we have shut anyone outside our heart. If we discover one locked out in anger, resentment or hurt, we open our heart in forgiveness......We allow the breath of the Spirit to breath in us. With each gentle breath, We are filled with love and peace. As we think of those we wish to forgive, we recognize in their reflection the same Spirit that is in you. At the level of spiritual knowing, we understand that we are all one...We release the judgements of our worldly thoughts and allow forgiveness to unite us in love. We are one in the wholeness of God, so we are one with all others..........

ONCE A UPON A MIDNIGHT CLEAR........

GOD's Love For US. . . .

Made in the USA
Columbia, SC
12 July 2021